For my girl.
My world.

About the author

Annie Woods (pseudonym) is the Author of My Kid Loves Broccoli – a blog about life with an amazing child (Hannah) who happens to have a rare genetic condition and Autism.

Annie lives in the North of England with her husband (aka Daddy Broccoli), daughter Hannah, and Hannah's assistance dog, gentle Jade.

Annie is passionate (well… slightly obsessed, really) about raising awareness of Hannah's condition. She dreams of upping sticks and setting up a charity in Cornwall – providing luxury holidays and therapeutic interventions for disabled kids and their families, whilst tending to her organic walled garden and bunch of alpacas (not too much to ask, really, is it?).

Annie loves writing, art, crisps, alcohol and swearing sometimes. *coughs* Well, quite a lot, really.

She is also Daniel Craig's Plan B …although he doesn't know it… yet.

The (little) Book of Broccoli

by Annie Woods

First published in Great Britain in 2021 by
Words are Life
10 Chester Place,
Adlington, Chorley, PR6 9RP
wordsarelife@mail.com
www.wordsarelife.co.uk

Electronic version and paperback versions available for purchase on Amazon.

Doodles and Stuff About Our Rare Journey
by
Annie Woods

Welcome!
Come on in.
No.
Don't bother wiping your feet.
Shift those toys and make
yourself comfy.

I'll put the kettle on.

Fancy a biscuit?
Oh, best to avoid the ones with
raisins in.

...I'll explain later.

Intro

I didn't actually plan to write this book (Blimey, I'd never get a job in sales or marketing with that pitch).

I was actually in the throes of writing The Book of Broccoli… a book about our life with a child who has a rare genetic condition.

In 2020 all our lives changed… and I had so many plans too…

Typical!

I gave up my profession to start my own business, spend more time writing and support Hannah through her first year of high school, then a world pandemic turned up and life was put on hold whilst I became a full-time stay-at-home-mum/teacher/entertainer/nurse/therapist etc etc and etc.

What spare time was afforded me, just to keep me ever so slightly sane, I continued writing. Then, when things got tough, I veered away from the words and got a bit carried away doodling - so much so, that I ended up with a book of doodles!

So, whilst everyone's (very patiently) waiting for me to get my act together and finish the one that was supposed to be first, I thought I'd get this one published.

I really do hope you like it.

Naturally, it doesn't (and can't possibly) reflect every aspect of my life as a mummy to a child with profound disabilities. But perhaps may give you a bit of taster.

It's important to note that everyone's experiences differ...

These are just ours.

OUR STORY...

I saw them.

Just the two of them,
walking hand in hand
on the beach.
Mother and child...
...and, for the first
time, it struck me.

I'll never have that.

Doctors said that pregnancy was "highly unlikely".

But the 'unlikely' happened!

I had all these
wonderful

as to how our life
would be.

I'd help her do whatever she wanted.

We could dress up and go for fancy afternoon tea somewhere.

Just the two of us.

We could go on adventures together.

We could
go exploring
in
rock pools.

...and then she
arrived...

All my dreams
were shattered.

I felt like
my world
had turned
upside down.

Medical staff buzzed around day and night.

They said she was
very poorly.

She was tested...
and tested...
and tested...

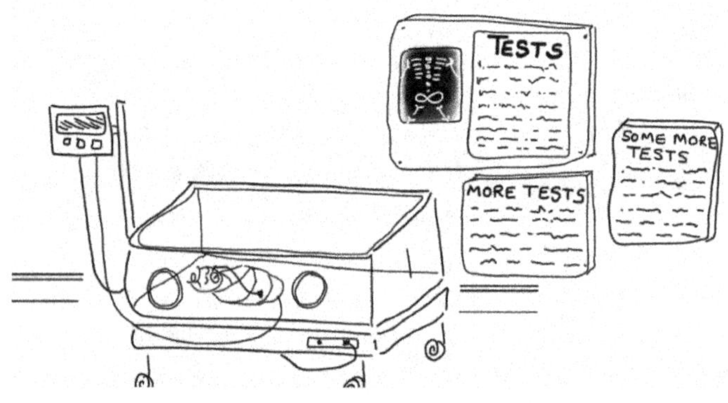

Her new environment
was never peaceful.
**BEEP. BEEP. BEEP.
BEEP. BEEP.**

When I needed a check
up, they sent me to
the maternity ward.

Surrounded by happy
mummies with happy,
healthy babies, I
felt like the
elephant in the room.
...and it felt cruel
and thoughtless too.

There was no
provision for me to
stay with her
overnight.

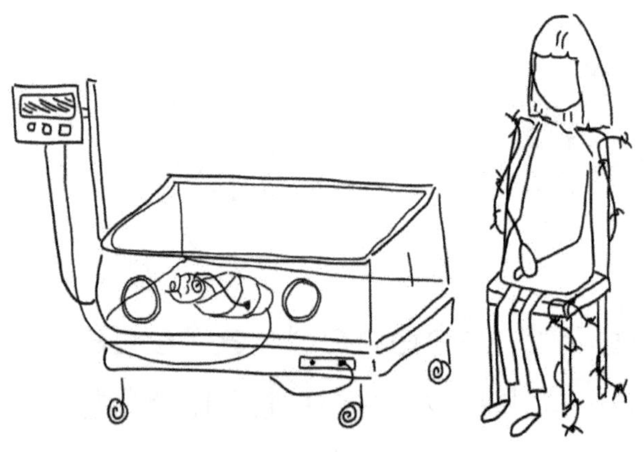

But, during the day,
they gave me a chair
to sit on.
It felt like sitting
on barbed wire. (I'd
been stitched,
unpicked, then
stitched again.)

Someone
I knew
offered
to buy the
ward a new chair.

They said no,
because of
"health and safety".

But parents
have needs
too.

I feel
these get
forgotten
sometimes.

They said they
were worried about
her heart.

So she went for a
ride in an ambulance
to get it checked
out.

They told me
she had
two holes
in her heart
and a heart defect
that couldn't
be fixed.

My own heart
was broken.

As the days went by,
the list of concerns
grew...
and grew...
and grew...

Without having
the answers,
they told me
all kinds of
speculative stuff –
that she'd never do
X,Y,Z.

We then went to
see the wonderful
and clever
Genetics people.

They told me
she had…

...although it took a
further seven years
for the outcome of
which specific gene
was affected.

Cornelia de Lange syndrome (or CdLS) is a very rare condition, affecting 1 in 30,000 individuals - from mild to severe.

There is no cure, but there are treatment guidelines which can help manage the syndrome.

It's considered a Rare Disease (but you can't catch it!)

CdLS is caused by a
change in 1 of 7
genes.

Research is carried
out all over the
world.

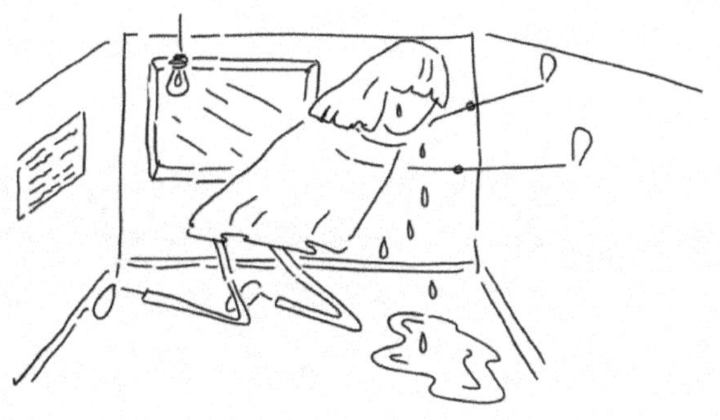

...and the room closed
in on me...

I thought our lives,
now so inextricably
linked, were over.

Why me?
Why her?

Well, why not us?

The blue skies seemed
to have gone.

They welcomed me to Holland*.

It didn't feel like Holland.

*Welcome to Holland is an essay written by Emily Perl Kingsley in 1987 about the experience of having and raising a child with a disability.

It felt like
I'd landed
on the moon.

There was a lot of crying in the shower.

It felt like our home
was being invaded
every day.

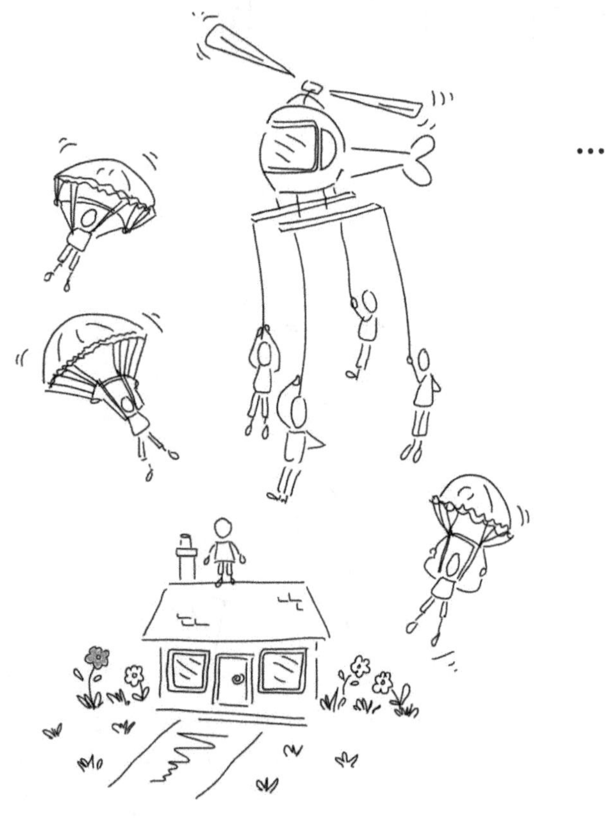

but they were just
trying to do their
job.

ALL. THE. STUFF.

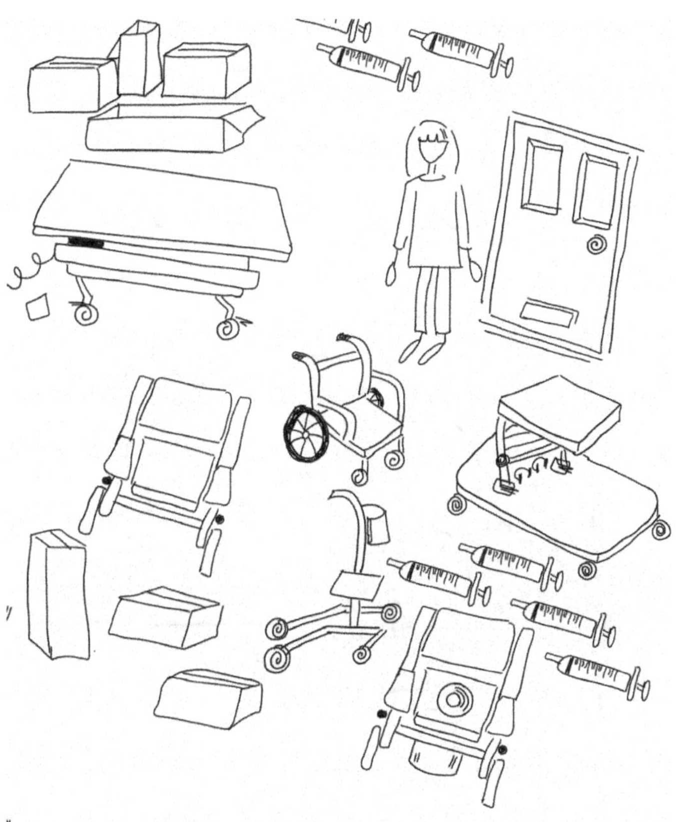

...overwhelming,
but necessary!

I didn't recognise myself anymore.

...But then,
with time,

I did.

I found my feet
eventually.

(I only have two,
btw).

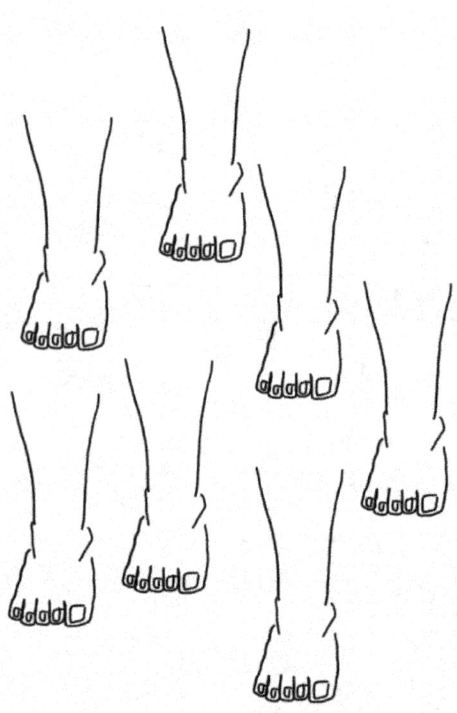

In the 1940's,
Professor Theodore
Woodward advised his
medical students when
diagnosing patients
to think of horses
and not zebras when
they heard hoofbeats.

That they should
consider what is more
common, rather than
something exotic.

In medicine, the term "Zebra" is often used to refer to a Rare Disease (of which there are 7,000).

Everyone has their own unique stripes. Just like a zebra.

(A group of zebras is called a dazzle!)

If you've met one person with Cornelia de Lange Syndrome (CdLS), you've done just that...

Met one person.

She had such
difficulty
swallowing. Learning
to do it was scary at
times. The tube that
went up her nose and
into her tummy kept
her alive.

But with time
and patience, she
mastered it.

There were many scary times...

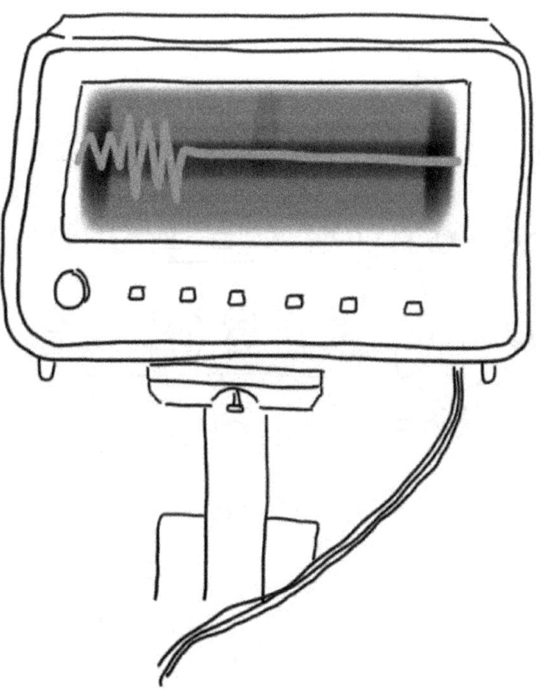

But we   got
through them
together.

"YOU never know how
strong you are until
being STRONG
is the only choice
you have"

Bob Marley

Some of the firsts were initially difficult (for me)

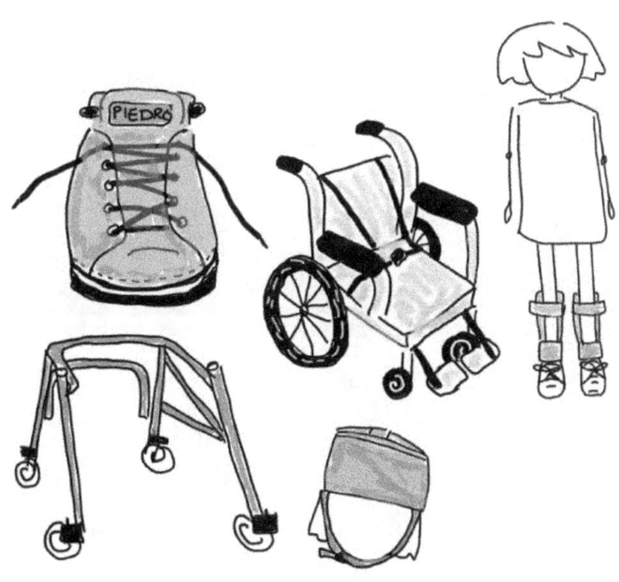

Letting go was hard.

Still is…

It's a roller-coaster life!

She's non-verbal, but she still wants to communicate.
There's many ways of doing it.

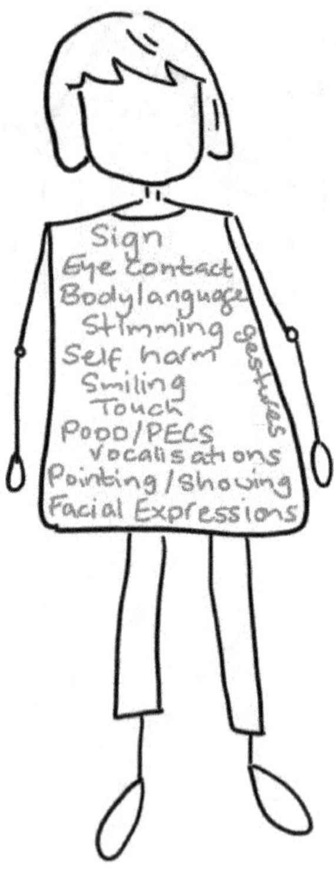

All behaviour is
communication.

She can't tell me how
her day has been.

I've wished I was a
fly on the wall.

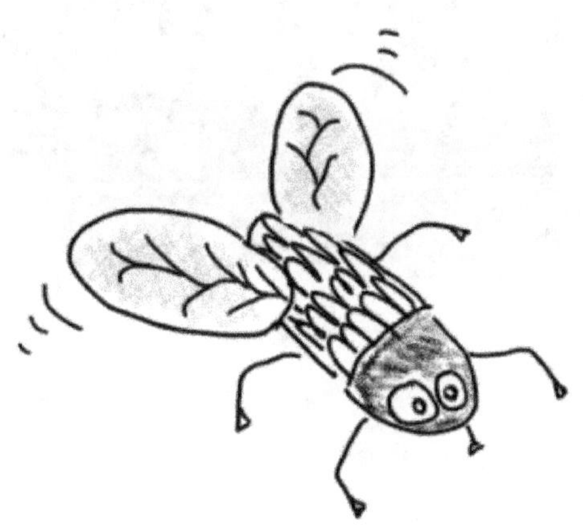

I'm still
waiting to
hear the
word...

When she was two
years old she
couldn't even sit up
on her own.

But with lots of help
from a charity...

...and a HUGE amount of
tenacity.

...she took her first wobbly steps eighteen months later.

Yay!

It was THE best Christmas present... ever!

Small steps matter.

They really do!

I wished I could find
a magic key to unlock
all that potential.

Never underestimate the importance of asking for help.

(There's no shame in asking!)

And never
underestimate the
power of both
listening and
being heard.

The Death Stare...

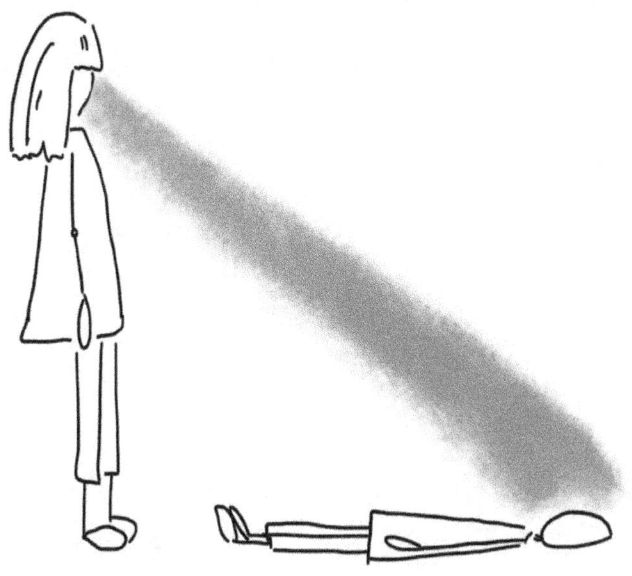

...is only ever put
into operation just
prior to mummy losing
her sh*t.

Said Death Stare is reserved solely for adults who fail to do their jobs properly (and is used only in the best interests of her poppet).

Be afraid of the Death Stare.

Be very, very afraid!

So many mountains we climb...

Sometimes we
slip down...

But reaching the top feels amazing!

There's still lots of climbing to do.

People say that she's
tough, resilient,
brave.

That she copes.

That she's a fighter.

And she's all of that
and much, much more.

But that also makes
my heart hurt as
she's never been
given another option.

She's just a kid.

A kid who's had to experience things in her short life that many other people will never have to.

Celebrating achievements...

They say "It's the small things that matter"...

...but to us, they're not small.
They're often HUGE!

Sometimes
it can feel
a lonely place...

The starers suck!

You learn who GENUINELY cares!

UGH!

I don't know how you do it
BLAH
God only sends special children to special people
BLAH
She'll be okay
BLAH
She's not like a normal child
God only gives you what you can handle
BLAH
BLAH
I'm Sorry
BLAH
BLAH

It'd be a wise move
not to tell me how to
tie my laces:

a. Unless I ask.

b. If you've never
walked in my
shoes.

"I know"

Two words that can either infuriate me or give me the warm fuzzies.

If you've never lived something, you can't possibly know how it can feel.

It's important to
find your Tribe

The ones who
completely 'get it'.

Your Tribe could be
half way across the
world...

But they're there
for you
in a click!

There's a sense of
humour that only
Special Parents
understand.

...probably.

There are holes to get stuck in.

They'll say

Fill this form in…

We don't have a
service…

It isn't possible…

We can't provide
that…

You must look after
yourself…

It must be hard, but
we're thinking of
you…

There's a long wait…

Whilst they continue
to watch you in the
hole.

From afar…

But there's often a fellow Special Parent who will come to the rescue!

Special mums do better research than the FBI and MI6 put together!

Knowledge
is
power.

We're experts at finding solutions...

And there's
one thing we
now know:
TRUST.
YOUR.
GUT.

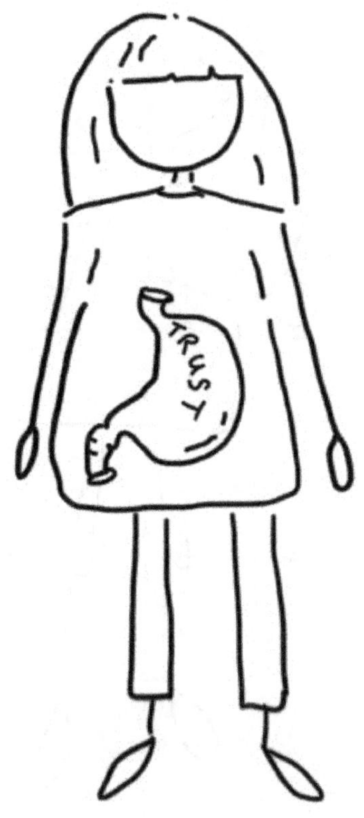

Big reports with fancy words and medical jargonese can feel daunting at first...

You soon become an expert in your child's strengths and needs...

Even when you're overwhelmed by

ALL.
THE.
PAPERWORK.

Annie Woods

AND.
ALL.
THE.
APPOINTMENTS.

Ugh!
(But they're
necessary.)

Although there are times when everything feels like tick box exercises, rather than meaningful intervention.

It's
a
bit
of
a
juggling
act

There's been quite a
bit of lifting and
carrying to do over
the years...

Believe me.

Hiding away from it
all really isn't an
option...

There's so much
to consider...

"The List"

ALWAYS presented to
the newbies in charge
of her care.

Lack of sleep...

95

SHE.
LOVES.
FOOD.

...especially
broccoli.

Annie Woods

She has no
awareness
of
keeping safe.

Having eyes in the back of your head...

...is not optional!

It's a
sensory thing.

A group of people is called a "no thanks".

BUT

Thank you to the professionals who GENUINELY want to make a difference.

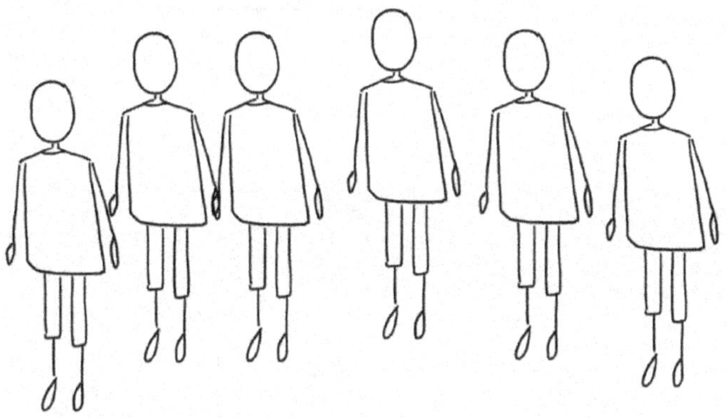

...we can suss you a mile off!

Don't let the system
get you down.
We value you... very
much.

You, and the little
rays of sunshine that
help make life just a
bit easier.

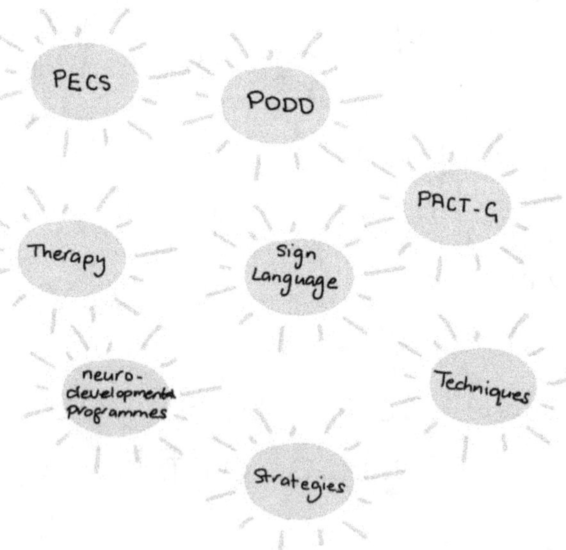

Okay, pop pickers, in at number 1 in the album charts for the last consecutive 8 years is SEND Mama with The Broken Record...

...featuring top hits such as:

- Be careful!

- Stop!

- Don't lick that!

- Take it out! (of your mouth)

  And, never forgetting...

- Don't drink the bath water!

  Nice.

red tape sucks!

There are times you have to kick the barriers down!

There are times when you must fight!

(figuratively speaking, obvs.)

Especially
when your child
doesn't fit their
criteria.

Assertiveness and confidence are required!

And you have to
Speak up!

With challenge
comes change!
Think outside
the box...

...or better still,
get rid of the box!

Routines - essential

Change - challenging

Assessment - crucial

Support - vital

Intervention - early

Communication - key

Inclusion -
fundamental

Solutions - sought

We're made to feel like it's begging...

And there appears to be an assumption that SEND parents ought to spill their guts to everyone about everything.

Btw, we don't have a cat.

In 2020/2021 the world got a taster of social isolation

Families, just like mine, have been doing it for years.

...no they don't!

True Story!

FML
W.C.
CLOSED
(Because we don't
want homeless
people using it)
Oink oink

THANK GOD FOR CHANGING PLACES!

I am the potty time
supervisor...

...so I suspect
she's returning
the favour!

Reflux doesn't
discriminate as to
where it strikes.

And I'm winning at
life after mastering
the art of discreetly
catching it in my
hands.
Go me!

Late!

...regardless of what time we get up.

All the road trips.

They're always only two minutes... *rolls eyes*

My girl is the greatest teacher!

She taught me all
about unconditional
love.

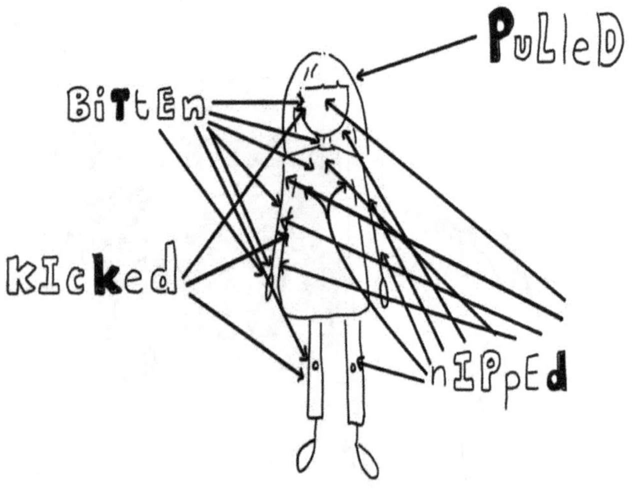

Our Special Biscuit Recipe

We don't share perfect Insta photos of our perfect Insta family, doing perfect Insta baking in our perfect Insta kitchen.

That's not real life anyway.

We do messy, mostly, but we have fun doing it.

Here's one of our favourite recipes.

Ingredients

100g butter
50g caster sugar
150g self-raising flour
Bowl of raisins

Method

* Dramatically tip butter into a bowl. Actually, just throw butter bowl into the other bowl. It's quicker.

* Using a teaspoon that you've licked already, slowly scoop sugar into the butter. Bash the spoon against the bowl of sugar so as to burst everyone's ear drums… including the dog's.

* Rub spoon in your hair.

* Throw spoon into bowl.

* Get your assistant (mummy) to
fish spoon out. Throw spoon
into bowl again. Get assistant
to fish spoon out. Mix
ingredients twice
anticlockwise, then get your
assistant to do the rest of the
mixing whilst you rub your
buttered hands on your top.

* Add flour. Mix - same method
as above.

* Get assistant to split
ingredients into 16 walnut
sized clumps, whilst you rub
ingredients into your trousers.

* Place on baking trays x 2.

* Squish down with fork,
alternating between squishing
down ingredients, putting fork
in mouth, trying to comb hair
with it, and flicking
ingredients around the room.
Laugh hysterically.

* Find bowl of raisins. Eat most of them quickly. Suck a raisin then place one on each biscuit. Sometimes chew raisin before sucking and placing on biscuit.

* Get assistant to place in preheated oven (160 fan) for 15 - 20 mins whilst you bite your hand off in frustration because you can't eat biscuits immediately.

* Throw some toys around for a bit.

* Once cooked and cooled, stuff as many biscuits in your face as you can.

You. Are. Welcome!

I'm SO proud of her!

...although I was slightly less so when she threw baby Jesus on the floor in the school nativity...

...and when she opened
all His presents off
the three Kings
IN FRONT OF
THE WHOLE SCHOOL.

#cringe

We may have
similarities, but
we're all unique.

We all blossom at
different times… and
in different ways.

Different,
not less!

I want her to believe in herself.

Childhood shouldn't
be a competition –
who did what first.

Have you ever had to
disclose the date of
when you were potty
trained on a job
application?

I rest my case.

Let kids be kids.

As she grew, I couldn't keep her wrapped in cotton wool for long...

...she needed adventures!

Walking
with alpacas…

(His name was Ziggy.)

Winning Awards!

Riding on zip wires...

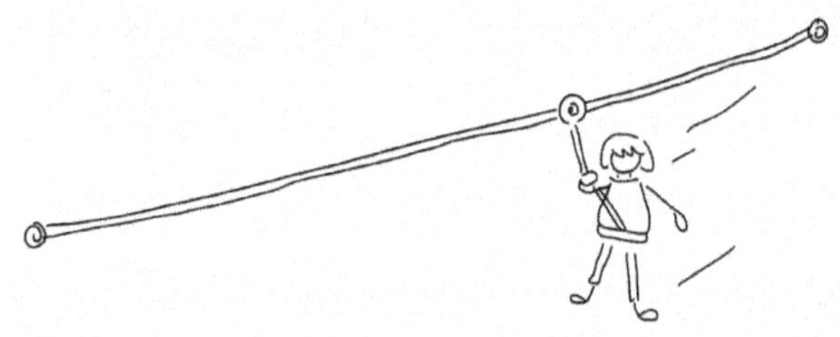

Representing her school in sports competitions…

(Boccia)

Raising money for other people who need help...

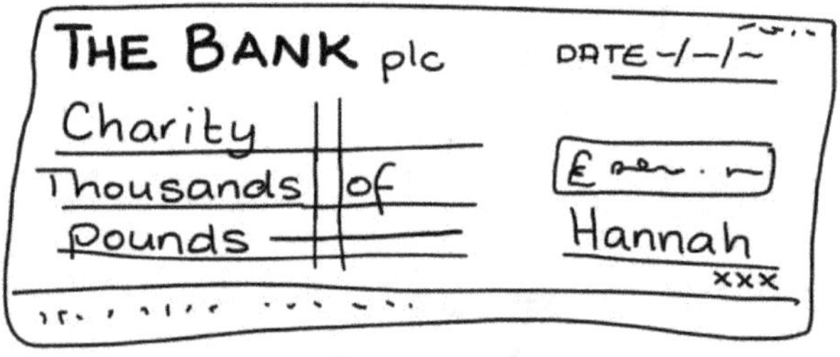

INCLUSION MATTERS!
INCLUSION MATTERS!
INCLUSION MATTERS!
INCLUSION MATTERS!
INCLUSION MATTERS!
INCLUSION MATTERS!
INCLUSION MATTERS!
INCLUSION MATTERS!
INCLUSION MATTERS!
INCLUSION MATTERS!
INCLUSION MATTERS!
INCLUSION MATTERS!
INCLUSION MATTERS!
INCLUSION MATTERS!

What others see...

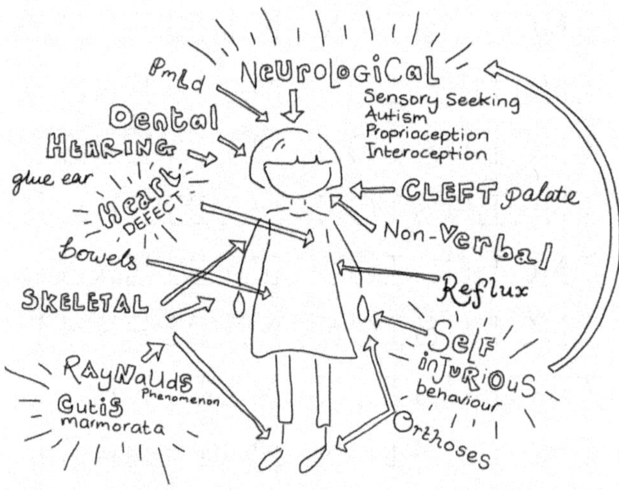

But...

...I wish they could
see her like I do.

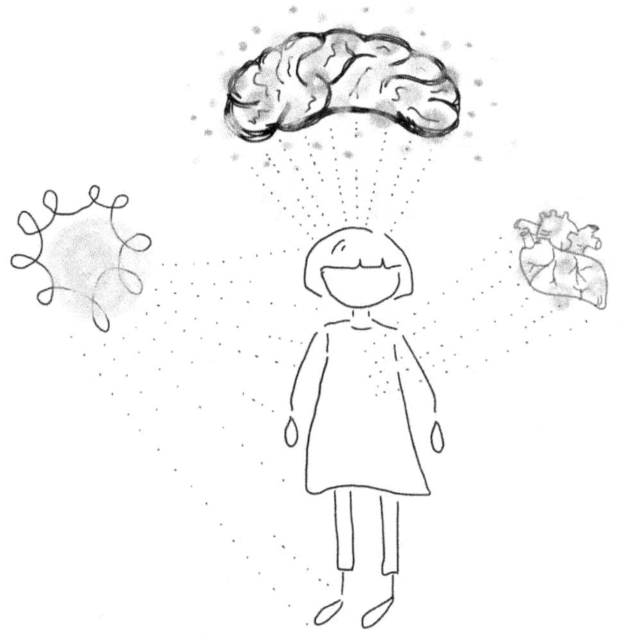

She has THE most AMAZING eyelashes!

Answers on a postcard, please...

Sometimes, things can feel just a bit rubbish.

147

It's okay to
feel the feels.

It's okay to
say you're not okay.

It's okay to
say you are okay.

**Denial
Anger
Bargaining
Depression
Acceptance**

No order, no
timescale, and not
necessarily all of
the above (but
hopefully
acceptance!)

Just don't
get stuck.

Seek help.

It isn't good to bottle things up.

I

We often
feel
invisible.

They can come from any angle...

The unnecessary assumptions.

The unnecessary speculation.

The unnecessary flippant remarks.

We can be subjected to them time and time and time again.

AND.
IT.
IS.
DRAINING!

People seem to think they can say whatever they want to

...because it's 'well meaning'

THE TYPEWRITER of TRUTHS

Sometimes, I just
need to vent.

We find ourselves
saying we're okay
when we're
probably not.

Low battery: recharge necessary!

Just so you know, NONE OF THIS IS 'ME TIME'

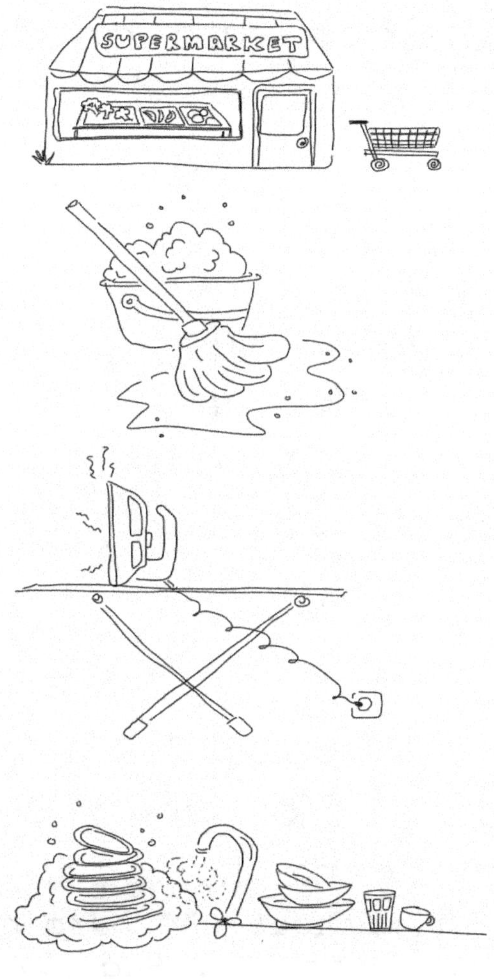

It's going to the chippy with your BFF. Ordering chips, curry and a can of dandelion and burdock and sitting in the park...

...

just like when you were kids.
(But without the burping competitions. Sadly.)

It's a coffee and a chat with friends...

Bath Time, Me Time!

Huzzah for coffee and booze!

TOTALLY winging mummyhood.

When
challenges
come,
just
remember,
take...

ONE

dAy

@ a

TiMe

NEVER
SAY
NEVER

...EVER!

We still want
to be
invited...

...but we
might not
be able
to come.

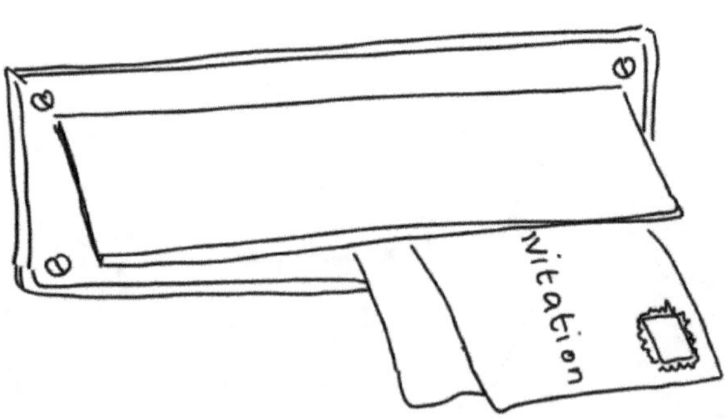

The list of people
I'd trust to care for
my child is so small,
you'd need to read it
with one of these.

Our dog, Jade,
is an expert
at helping
to take
socks off.

Friends who
want to
spend time
with her
are
so precious.

God
bless
grandparents.

Just going out
for a
few hours
can feel like
packing
to go on
holiday.

There's lots of
things to remember.

We do have
PERFECT DAYS
though...

It's all
fun and games
until you're
dodging the
dog poo.

Guys, pick up
after your dogs…
you dirty buggers!

Other parents
can hurt…
The way they clutch
their poppets close
as we approach.

We DO notice!

…and,
for the record,
we're NOT
infectious.
But they
might be!

We can clear a playground in minutes… without doing anything. It's great!

We may not have everything, but we have...

Oodles of it!

We know all about
the importance
of living
in the
here and now...

...and trying not to
dwell too much
on the future.

People often
ask me
what the
future
will bring.

I don't know
...do you?

The thought of
leaving her
all alone
is just
unbearable
sometimes.

The thought
of being
without her
is more
unbearable.

I'll be
waiting for her.

We have NOW.

So we'd better
try and make
the most of it.

I was
mistaken.

Our lives
weren't over.

Not by any
means.

Acknowledgements

Huge massive thanks to you, dear reader, for taking an interest in the book. I really hope you liked it and got something out of it.

I very much hope you'll like my next book too. Although, just a heads up, it'll be much longer.

Much, much longer!

Massive thanks to my AMAZING Facebook Tribe, who have been ever so patient with me re: The Book of Broccoli (my next book – although Lord knows when I'll finish it!). I cannot thank you enough for all the support you've provided over the years. I feel extremely grateful that I consider many of you, no matter where you are in the world, my friends. Thanks too for celebrating with us (you have no idea how much that means), for the guidance and words of wisdom, for putting up with my gripes… and for the laughs.

You really are a smashing bunch!

Lesley, my very clever and talented publisher friend. Without whom, you wouldn't have this book in your hands…and for understanding and the gentle words of encouragement.

Mum, Dad, Harry…
I hope there's a bookshop in Heaven and you get to read this.

Daddy, I wished you'd have got the opportunity to meet her… you'd have loved her! My heart misses you all every day, but parts of you live on as you helped shaped me to be the person I am.

Love is eternal.

To Daddy Broccoli: Despite claiming not to have much interest in my blatherings over the years, I suspect he'll be just a tiny bit proud that his spouse has actually managed to have a book published and can now call herself an author.

Do let me know if you find out, please.

To the CdLS UK and Ireland Foundation for being there for us from day one. I truly don't know where we'd be without you all. Thanks just aren't enough.

...and, of course, our global CdLS family. You make me feel less alone. I'm sending you massive squishy hugs and all my love.

...and last, but certainly not least, **my precious girl**.

Without you my world would have no colour.

Keep going Tiger...you're doing great!

I hope you know how loved you are.

Forever, your mummy.

(oh, and thanks for loaning me your ipad!)

Useful Stuff

When I was just starting out on my own journey with a child who has CdLS, I came across some misinformation which scared me stiff.

I don't want that for anyone else.

So here are the sites which will provide accurate information regarding Cornelia de Lange:

www.cdls.org.uk

www.findresources.co.uk/the-syndromes/cornelia-de-lange/key-facts

www.cdlsworld.org

www.cdlsusa.org

And here's the first International Consensus Statement for the Diagnosis and Management of Cornelia de Lange Syndrome… written by THE experts!

www.nature.com/articles/s41576-018-0031-0

CdLS Awareness Day is celebrated annually (and globally) on the second Saturday of May.

Where to find us...

You can find us mostly lurking around Facebook. Just search for My Kid Loves Broccoli.

We're also on Insta and Twitter (although I wouldn't bother, tbh).

You can find my past blog post blatherings on
www.mykidlovesbroccoli.wordpress.com

I haven't written on there for such a long time. Too long, really. Because, life and all that. But there are plenty posts on there for you to peruse.

Come join the Tribe.

This Is Not

The End

www.ingramcontent.com/pod-product-compliance
Lightning Source LLC
Chambersburg PA
CBHW051515030726
47592CB00006B/2285